Citizen Dog

by Mark O'Hare

WARNER BOOKS

A *Warner* Book

First published in Great Britain in 1999 by Warner Books

Copyright © 1998 by Mark O'Hare

Citizen Dog is a cartoon feature created by Mark O'Hare and syndicated internationally by Universal Press Syndicate. *Citizen Dog* was first published in the United States by Andrews McMeel Publishing, an Andrews McMeel Universal Company, Kansas City, Missouri.

The moral right of the author has been asserted.

A CIP catalogue record for this book is available from the British Library.

ISBN 0 7515 2682 7

Printed and bound in Great Britain by Bath Press Ltd.

Warner Books. A division of Little, Brown and Company (UK), Brettenham House, Lancaster Place, London WC2E 7EN

For Julie

Foreword

by Kevin Fagan

I laughed so hard at **Citizen Dog** one day that I actually got the hiccups. It's true! To get rid of them, I had to drink water through a straw while plugging my ears and holding my nose. I don't know where that remedy came from originally, but my grandma taught it to me, and now I'm passing it along to my fellow **Citizen Dog** fans. We may need it from time to time!

From the moment I saw **Citizen Dog**, I loved it. In case the strip is brand new to you, it's the story of a man and his dog. Or maybe it's the other way around. I haven't quite figured out which one is in charge. All I know is, Mel and Fergus are a great comedy team. Their relationship is kind of hard to explain, though. Let's just say it's more complicated than normal.

Mark O'Hare has a wonderful drawing style to go along with his amazing cleverness. His work never fails to brighten the day a little. **Citizen Dog** is new on the scene. But after reading this book, you may feel like it's been part of your life forever. I have a hunch that it will be.

— Kevin Fagan,
creator of **Drabble**

13

WHAT DRIVES A DOG,
TO DO WHAT HE DO,
WHEN HIS HEAD'S OUT DA WINDOW,
TO SEE WHO IS WHO?

DOES HE DO IT TO PLEASE,
HIS EARS IN THE BREEZE?
OR MAYBE TO FIND,
THAT DOG STATE OF MIND!

IS HE TEMPTING THE WIND, TO FILL UP HIS SOUL?

OR CHALLENGING FATE, TO SWALLOW HIM WHOLE ?!?

YET ONE QUESTION REMAINS,
WHEN WE ASK HOW HE FEEL,
IF HIS HEAD'S OUT THE WINDOW...

... WHO'S AT DA WHEEL ?

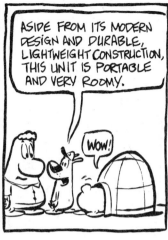

27

28

DOGS CAN PICK UP A VARIETY OF BAD HABITS. 	TO RE-ESTABLISH CONTROL, IT IS IMPERATIVE THAT YOU DISCOVER THE SOURCE OF HIS NEGATIVE BEHAVIOR. 		IF HE'S MADE IT TO CHAPTER FIVE, IT MAY BE TOO LATE. 

MC HARE

IF HE WON'T OBEY, TRY REASONING WITH HIM. / YOU MUST BE FIRM AT ALL TIMES. 	REMEMBER, A LITTLE DIPLOMACY CAN GO A LONG WAY. / LOOK HIM STRAIGHT IN THE EYE AND TELL IT LIKE IT IS. 	WILL YOU **PLEASE** STOP CHEWING THE DRAPES. / NO. 	HE MAY BE BELLIGERENT. KEEP TRYING! / HE'LL TRY THE DIPLOMACY ANGLE.. DON'T GO FOR IT. 

MC HARE

YOU MIGHT WANT TO CONSIDER OPENING UP MORE TO YOUR HOUSEMATE. 	LETTING DOWN YOUR WALL AND ADMITTING A PARTICULAR FAULT OF YOUR OWN IS ALWAYS A GOOD START. 	I'VE BEEN A LITTLE TOO IMPATIENT WITH YOU. / I'VE BEEN USING YOUR TOOTHBRUSH. 	IT'S AMAZING WHAT A DIFFERENCE A LITTLE COMMUNICATION CAN MAKE. 

MC HARE

YOU SEE, ARLO, FINDING THE PERFECT SPOT TO BURY YOUR BONE IS THE KEY.

ONCE YOU KNOW WHERE THAT IS, THE REST IS EASY.

BUT HOW DO YOU KNOW?

OH... YOU'LL KNOW.

YOU BETTER NOT SCREW UP ANYTHING DOWN THERE!

OH, SETTLE DOWN.

I'M NOT JUST INDISCRIMINATELY DIGGING UP DIRT WITH NEITHER DIRECTION NOR PURPOSE, MINING A HOLE TO NOWHERE.

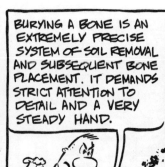

BURYING A BONE IS AN EXTREMELY PRECISE SYSTEM OF SOIL REMOVAL AND SUBSEQUENT BONE PLACEMENT. IT DEMANDS STRICT ATTENTION TO DETAIL AND A VERY STEADY HAND.

WHOOPS!

WHAT HAPPENED?

WELL, THAT'S A BUSTED WATER MAIN, MEL.

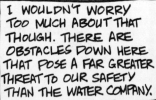

I WOULDN'T WORRY TOO MUCH ABOUT THAT THOUGH. THERE ARE OBSTACLES DOWN HERE THAT POSE A FAR GREATER THREAT TO OUR SAFETY THAN THE WATER COMPANY.

KA-BOOM!

THE GAS COMPANY, FOR INSTANCE.

OK! I'LL PLAY YOU GUYS, BUT TWO ON ONE IS UNFAIR!

YA GOTTA SET ME UP WITH SOMEONE TO EVEN OUT THE ODDS A LITTLE, RIGHT?

OHHH-NO! NO-NO-NO-NO-NO-NO-NO-NO-NO-NO-NO-NO-NO-NO-

OH BOY! OH, BOY! OH, BOY!

IT'S NOT FAIR AND YOU GUYS KNOW IT!

AWWW... COME ON, LARRY!

THE CAT'S NOT THAT BAD. HE'S JUST A LITTLE ENTHUSIASTIC.

LOOK AT HIM! HE'S HAVING A BLAST. BESIDES, I THINK HE REALLY WANTS TO PLAY.

WEEE!

CAN I BE QUARTERBACK?

OHHHH-NO NO-NO-NO-NO-NO-NO-NO-

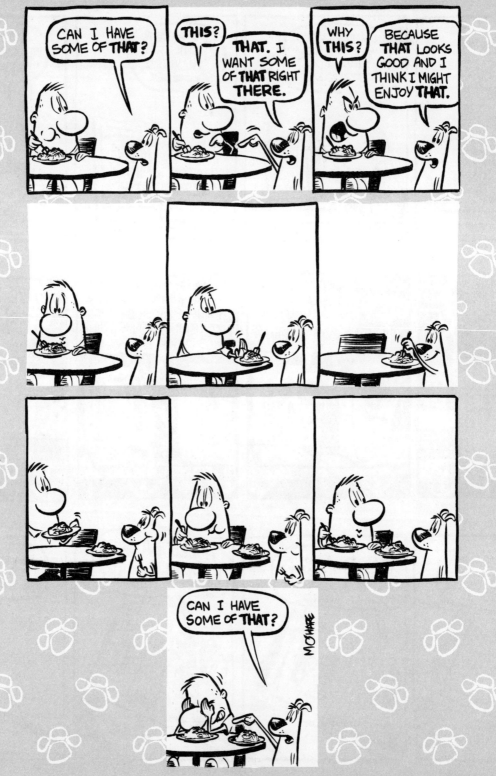

50

THEY'RE REAL PROFESSIONALS WHEN IT COMES TO THE SIMPLE THINGS.

DING!

DING!

SOME FOLKS LIKE TO LEAVE, THEIR ROMANCE TO FATE....

OR USE THOSE COMPUTERS, TO SEE HOW THEY RATE....

BUT I DON'T NEED GIMMICKS, TO LOOK UP MY MATE....

JUST GIMME A DOG PARK, TA FIND ME A DATE!

"AT OWN RISK!"

HE THINKS YOU GOT NICE—

WHAM! WHAM! WHAM! WHAM! WHAM! WHAM! WHAM!

WHAT'D I SAY?!

WILL YOU PLEEEASE LET ME DO THE TALKING.

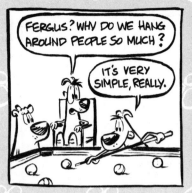

61

70

77

80

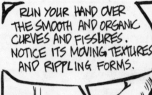

I'M NOT HERE TO ASK FOR ANYTHING.

I'VE BEEN PRETTY BAD THIS YEAR AND BOTH YOU AND I KNOW THAT I WON'T BE GETTING ANY PRESENTS.

IS THIS REAL?

SECURITY!!

ALL THE DRAPES ARE SHREDDED, SO I'LL NEED SOME OF THOSE... AND NEW CARPETING IN THE HALL WHERE HE TORE THAT HOLE.

AND CALL MRS. LAWRENCE'S LAWYER TO SEE IF SHE'LL SETTLE OUT OF COURT. I'D BE HAPPY TO PAY ALL OF HER MEDICAL BILLS.

SHE HAD THE RESTRAINING ORDER LAST YEAR. REMEMBER THAT?

WHERE DO YOU PEOPLE COME FROM?

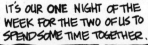

SO HOW DID THIS HAPPEN?

HOW DO ANY OF THESE THINGS HAPPEN, FERGUS?

YOU LOOK AWAY FOR A SECOND, OR TAKE A WRONG TURN...AND **WHAM!**...THE WORLD JUST SWALLOWS YOU UP. IT'S ALL PART OF THE DELICATE BALANCE OF NATURE.

CINNAMON OR SPEARMINT?

SPEARMINT.

ZIP!

IN THE END, YOU JUST GOTTA LEARN TO PICK YOURSELF UP AND MAKE THE BEST OF A BAD SITUATION.

I'M LOOKIN' OVERRR, MAH DEAD DOG ROVERRR...

...THAT I LEFT STRANDED IN THE STREEET....

TWANG TWANG TWANG

BLESS YOU, MA'AM!

YOU AIN'T NOTHIN' BUT A HOUND DOG, CRYIN' ALL THE TIME...

...YOU AIN'T NEVER CAUGHT A RABBIT AN' YOU AIN'T NO FRIEND A' MINE!

STRUM STRUM STRUM...

THANK YEWWWW... THANK YEWWWW...

I'M **NOT** LEAVIN' 'TILL YOU PAY FOR THOSE!

PAY FOR THESE? HA!

MUNCH MUNCH MUNCH

THERE'S NO WAY I'M GONNA HELP FUND AN OUTDATED SOCIALIST INSTITUTION THAT STUNTS THE INDIVIDUALISM AND FREE THINKING OF THIS COUNTRY'S PRECIOUS YOUTH.

MUNCH MUNCH MUNCH

.. MUNCH MUNCH MUNCH MUNCH

WELCOME TO GLUTTON BURGER, MAY I TAKE YOUR ORDER?

UH... LETS SEEE... I'LL HAVE—

OHHH... I DON'T CARE. JUST GIMME EVERYTHING TO THE LEFT OF BACON CHEESEBURGER!

HEY, MAN. I AIN'T PICKY.

THANK YOU. THAT'LL BE $63.50.

MEL! MEL! HE'S MY MAN!! IF HE WON'T GIMME SOME, NO ONE CAN!!

SHOOKA SHOOKA SHOO SHOO

YYYYEAAY MEL!

WOO! ALL RIGHT, MEL! YEAH!

MEL

"A" FOR EFFORT.

THAT'S THE SPIRIT!

YOU GOT ONE, TOO!

MAN AND DOG! A RELATIONSHIP AS OLD AS TIME ITSELF.

RENALDO!

THIS WEEK ON "RENALDO," WE'LL BE EXPLORING THE WONDER AND MAGIC OF THIS DEVOTED COUPLE AND TRY TO FIND—

DON'T START WITH ME!!

WHAT?! WHAT?!

ROWA!

RENALDO!

SO, FELLAS! EXACTLY HOW DO YOU KEEP THE MAGIC ALIVE?

RENAL!

WELL, RENALDO, IT'S THIS EXTRAORDINARY UNSPOKEN LOYALTY BETWEEN US THAT GROWS AND EVOLVES AND—

IT'S THOSE LITTLE SAUSAGE BISCUIT THINGIES.

I'LL STICK AROUND AS LONG AS HE KEEPS ....FEEDING... ME...THOSE...

WHAT HE SAID.

BREATHMINTS?
AISLE THREE.

HEY REGGIE! HOW'S IT GOIN'?
TERRIBLE!

I SLIPPED ANOTHER DISC, MY KIDNEYS DECIDED TO TAKE A VACATION AND I KEEP LOSIN' MY GLASSES.

I'M LOSIN' IT!! I'M FALLIN' APART!! I COULD GO AT ANY MINUTE, I'M TELLIN' YA!

WELL, COULD YA HANG ON JUST ONE MORE DAY FOR ME?
OHHH...I SUPPOSE.
SKRITCH SKRITCH SKRITL

SO HOW WAS YOUR WEEK?
LOUSY!

LOUSY BATHS, LOUSY NATURE WALKS AND UNBELIEVABLY LOUSY FOOD!

NOT TO MENTION EVERYBODY KEEPS TREATIN' ME LIKE A COMPLETE NINCOMPOOP.

SOUNDS LIKE MY WEEK!
OH.. A COMEDIAN.

PING!

WHAT AN UNBELIEVABLE PERFORMANCE MEL HAS PUT ON FOR GOLF FANS TODAY!

HE IS ONLY ONE STROKE AWAY FROM CLINCHING THIS YEAR'S PISMO BEACH MILLION-DOLLAR PURSE...

...IF HE CAN JUST CLEAR THE WINDMILL.

HOLE THREE IS THE DREADED CASTLE KEEP! IT'S A PAR FIVE.

AIM FOR THE ASCENDING DRAWBRIDGE AND ANGLE YOUR BALL THROUGH THE CLOSING GATES.

BUT BEWARE! DON'T OVERSHOOT YOUR BALL INTO THE MOAT OR YOU'LL HAVE TO FACE THE FEROCIOUS MAN-EATING CROCODILES!

OOOHHHH... SCARY.

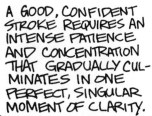

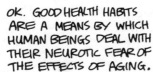